30 Minutes
... To Make the
Right Decision

Jane Smith

D1454976

KOGAN
PAGE

YOURS TO HAVE AND TO HOLD

BUT NOT TO COPY

First published in 1997
Reprinted 1998, 2000

Kogan Page Limited
120 Pentonville Road
London
N1 9JN

© Jane Smith, 1997

British Library Cataloguing in Publication Data
A CIP record for this book is available from the British Library.

ISBN 0 7494 2357 9

Typeset by Florencetype Ltd, Stoodleigh, Devon
Printed in England by Clays Ltd, St Ives plc

CONTENTS

The 30 Minutes Series

The *Kogan Page 30 Minutes Series* has been devised to give your confidence a boost when faced with tackling a new skill or challenge for the first time.

So the next time you're thrown in at the deep end and want to bring your skills up to scratch or pep up your career prospects, turn to the *30 Minutes Series* for help!

Titles available are:

30 Minutes Before Your Job Interview

30 Minutes Before a Meeting

30 Minutes Before a Presentation

30 Minutes to Boost Your Communication Skills

30 Minutes to Succeed in Business Writing

30 Minutes to Master the Internet

30 Minutes to Make the Right Decision

30 Minutes to Prepare a Job Application

30 Minutes to Write a Business Plan

30 Minutes to Write a Marketing Plan

30 Minutes to Write a Report

30 Minutes to Write Sales Letters

Available from all good booksellers.
For further information on the series, please contact:

Kogan Page, 120 Pentonville Road, London N1 9JN
Tel: 0171 278 0433 Fax: 0171 837 6348

INTRODUCTION

This book will help you to become a more effective manager by improving the quality of the decisions you make. Planning, problem solving, recruitment, improving efficiency, delegating, reducing errors and waste – all these depend on your being able to make and implement decisions effectively.

Decision-making skills and techniques underpin most aspects of management. The art of good decision making is complex, encompassing a wide range of personal and interpersonal skills. These include fact finding, logical thinking, creativity, analytical ability, sensitivity to others and assertiveness. Decision making also relies on a thorough knowledge of a variety of techniques and processes.

You can react to situations that require a decision in any one of four ways:

■ Put your head in the sand – ignore or avoid it

■ Act without thinking – do the first thing that comes into your head

- Positively decide to do nothing
- Take action only after you have gathered information and given the matter some thought.

The aim of this book is discuss some approaches that will help you to avoid the first two options and to practise either one of the latter two. *30 Minutes to Make the Right Decision* makes the point that there are no right or wrong ways to make decisions – just different approaches for different decisions. In many cases, it's not taking the decision that is difficult. The hard part is getting people to implement decisions and make them work. In the following pages we explain how your whole approach can have a profound effect on the extent to which others feel committed to decisions.

1

THE IMPORTANCE OF DECISION MAKING

Deciding something means making a choice or coming to a conclusion – and neither of those things is easy. Sometimes you have to make very difficult decisions: for example, whether or not to make someone redundant; or whether to bring in a working procedure that you know will be unpopular. But it's vital for managers to be able to make effective decisions because the well-being – and even survival – of an organisation depend almost entirely on the quality of its decision-making processes.

This first chapter will discuss what decisions are and how the process of making a decision relates to problem solving. It will also look at the different types of decision that you make and will help you to analyse how effective your decisions are at the moment.

What is a decision?

Many of our decisions are made and acted on in a split second – sometimes the process takes place so fast that we are hardly aware of it. But it's important to analyse what is happening and how we can improve the process because your decisions are the means by which you move your work on to achieve your tasks and goals, and the way in which you make decisions can determine the extent to which others are committed to the content of the decisions.

When you make a decision you are at a crossroads – having to select one option out of two or more alternatives. These options are usually limited by constraints; for example:

- The situation you are in now
- The situation you would like to be in, in the future
- Resources available
- What other people will accept
- The feasibility of different options
- The time factor.

> Identifying and weighing up these constraining factors correctly is one of the most important aspects of good decision making.

Is it a problem or a decision?

Before moving on to examine decisions in more detail, it will be useful to explore briefly the differences between problem solving and decision making. Although the two activities are very closely connected, they are not synonymous.

- Trivial decisions, such as making up your mind what to have for breakfast, can hardly be said to involve problems

- Although most problems involve making decisions, problem solving comprises much more than just selecting a suitable option.

You may well have to confront many kinds of problems as part and parcel of your daily and weekly routine. For instance, there may be safety problems, conflicts between people, low productivity, poor morale, a high rate of absenteeism or insufficient resources.

How you deal with a particular problem often depends on its relative urgency and importance. If you have to deal with a crisis, such as the breakdown of equipment or an accident, you will most likely make a quick decision by yourself. If, on the other hand, you have to deal with a problem that is important but not urgent, you will probably consult others before deciding what to do. A problem will become more urgent, but not more important, as time passes. So it's vital not to put off dealing with an important problem, because it may then turn into a crisis.

> Whereas a decision is choice between two or more options, a problem is something that is difficult to deal with or to solve. Problems are usually solved by making decisions.

What decisions do you make?

As a manager you have to make many different kinds of decisions – if you think about it, you will realise that you are making them virtually all the time. Some are to do with your day-to-day operation; others are more long term and strategic in nature.

Operational decisions

The operational level is concerned with how the different functions of the organisation – marketing, production, finance and so on – contribute to its strategic plan. The purpose of decision making at this level is to ensure that customers obtain what they want, when they want it.

Here some examples of operational decisions that you may have to make:

- How the department or function can contribute to long-term organisational goals
- How to allocate tasks and resources to achieve desired objectives
- How to solve problems or improve work processes.
- How to reorganise the workload when someone is on holiday
- What to do about a customer complaint
- What to do if someone regularly fails to come into work
- When and where to hold meetings and who should participate
- Who to select as a result of a recruitment process.

Strategic decisions

Strategy is to do with matching an organisation's activities to the environment within which it operates and to its resource capability. The decisions that you take at this level are likely to be concerned with the scope of the organisation's activities.

Here are some examples of strategic decisions that you may face:

- Clarifying the overall purpose and direction of the organisation
- Deciding on goals and objectives for the organisation, and on objectives for individual departments and teams
- Planning how to achieve these objectives
- Deciding which people and resources will be required to achieve them
- Monitoring plans and deciding what to do if things have not worked out as expected
- Deciding how to respond to competitor activity
- Looking for ways of improving performance.

Becoming more aware of the decisions you make will help you analyse the process. Do you carry the whole burden of decision making on your own shoulders? Or do you involve other people? Do you make the key decisions of the day in a planned and rational way beforehand? Or do you make each decision as it comes along? Do you depend on your intuition to help you decide? Or do you prefer to use logical thinking to help you make at an appropriate choice?

> The decisions that you make are vital to your effectiveness as a manager. They will be reflected in your performance and in the results you achieve.

Who makes the decisions?

When we group decisions according to who might have responsibility for making them, we end up with decisions which are routine, urgent, problematic or consultative.

11

Routine

These are ordinary decisions on a wide range of issues. It often saves time if these decisions are left to one person, usually a manager or leader.

Examples of routine decisions are:

- What should go into this report, and who should receive a copy?
- Shall I deal with the meeting notes before or after the report to the general manager?

Urgent

Some problems occur rapidly and may have serious consequences if not dealt with immediately. Again, a manager will often deal with these personally and explain or justify them later.

Examples of urgent decisions are:

- Someone is ill – how to cope with his or her workload?
- The project deadline is approaching faster than expected – how to revise schedules to get it completed on time?

Problematic

These sorts of decisions must be taken when a difficulty has emerged and there is no obvious solution. It can be useful for a management team or a cross-functional sub-group to focus on these, and experts from outside the team may be called in to give advice.

Examples of problematic decisions are:

- How to get trade union support for a new working arrangement
- A new product is not selling as well as anticipated – how are we going to deal with this?

Consultative

Other decisions that you make will affect a lot of people over a long period. It is often important to involve those who will be affected by the results of the decision. This may mean including a whole department or team in the decision-making process or again, consulting other people from outside.

Examples of consultative decisions are:

■ Arrangements for a retirement party

■ We want to introduce a newsletter. What do people want? What would interest them?

This classification is largely a matter of personal choice and will depend on the particular circumstances of the individual decision. Nevertheless, even if your interpretation is very subjective, doing the analysis will help you to select an appropriate way of tackling a particular decision.

> Knowing what type of decision you are dealing with will help you to decide who should make the decision, and how and when it should be made.

Programmed and unprogrammed decisions

Another way of classifying decisions is to distinguish between those that are programmed and those that are unprogrammed.

■ **Programmed** decisions are those that are relatively unimportant or repetitive and have procedures or pre-established criteria set up to deal with them. The risks

13

involved are not great and they can, therefore, be more easily delegated. An example of this type of decision would be the reordering of raw materials, or deciding whether or not a product is of a high enough standard. Programmed decisions are usually made lower down the organisation and are usually routine and structured. Those managers who have to make them will have fewer alternatives to choose between

- **Unprogrammed** decisions are those that are new and non-repetitive and where the risks involved are high. They occur in unusual or ill-defined situations where there are many possible courses of action. Deciding what to do about an outbreak of pilfering or whether or not to expand into a new market would be examples of unprogrammed decisions. As a general rule, unprogrammed decisions tend to be taken at a more senior level of management.

Why are decisions important?

Decisions involve a commitment to action; and the hardest step in achieving anything is making a true commitment. You know you have made a decision when it leads directly to action – and carrying out the action is often easier than making the decision itself. Although it is important to go through the processes we describe in these pages, it is also crucial not to labour forever over the decision. Research has shown that the most successful managers are those who can make decisions rapidly, because they are clear about their values and objectives.

The decisions that you make affect the people in your department or section, and may well have a ripple effect both in the wider organisation and beyond. In the same way, the decisions that other people make often have implications for you. The whole process is extremely complex because it is often impossible to know whether a decision was 'good' or 'bad' until all its effects have been felt some time later. It is in avoiding potential problems and making the most of opportunities that you need to use a whole battery of skills – including logical thinking, risk analysis, creativity and intuition.

> Decisions are important because they have the power to trigger the process of turning aspirations and goals into reality.

How effective are your decisions?

In this chapter we have started to unravel some of the factors involved in decision making. The problem is that there is often no one 'right' decision – there may be several options and we have to use all our analytical and managerial skills to select the best, or the least harmful. Another complication is that making a decision is part of a much wider process, including gathering information, generating options and analysing risk.

Because there are so many skills and techniques involved in decision making, there may be some that you already do quite well and others that you would find it valuable to work on. Use this table to help you identify ways in which the remainder of this book can best help you:

Do you:	Often	Sometimes	Never
1. Select the right method of making a decision?			
2. Involve members of your team whenever you can?			
3. Stop and think what you want the decision to achieve?			
4. Take steps to collect all the information you need to make an important decision?			
5. Know how to apply logical thinking when appropriate?			
6. Know how to apply creative thinking when appropriate?			
7. Use effective ways of weighing up the options and selecting the most suitable one?			
8. Make sure everyone knows about a decision that affects them?			
9. Check to see whether a decision is bringing the required results?			
10. Admit that you are wrong if the decision turns out to be a bad one?			

Making quick or difficult decisions is hard – in fact, this is probably the most challenging part of your role as a manager. However, this book should help you to make more effective decisions. If you ticked 'sometimes' or 'never' for:

- Questions 1 or 2, look carefully at Chapter 2 for information on different styles of decision making

- Questions 3 or 4, look carefully at Chapter 3 to find out more about setting objectives and collecting information

- Questions 5 or 6, look carefully at Chapter 4 to find out how to generate a range of options for decisions

- Questions 7, 8, 9 or 10, look carefully at Chapter 5 to find out how to evaluate options and implement decisions

2

STYLES OF DECISION MAKING

A key decision-making skill is knowing who should take the decision and when and how it should be taken. Traditionally, managers or leaders have assumed the authority to take decisions alone and to pass them down the line for implementation. Now, successful organisations often try to ensure that problematic or consultative decisions are made by appropriate work groups or management teams. Decisions made by the wrong people at the wrong time in the wrong way can have disastrous implications when they are implemented.

As well as discussing different management styles, the chapter looks briefly at rational and intuitive approaches to making decisions.

Beliefs about people

The decision-making style you adopt will depend to a great extent on your beliefs about people. Research carried out by the behavioural psychologist Douglas McGregor suggests that your attitude to the people you work with will have a profound effect on the extent to which you feel able to delegate decisions. McGregor found that there are two opposing groups of assumptions about people. He called these two extremes 'Theory X' and 'Theory Y'.

Theory X believes that most people:

- Are lazy and dislike hard work
- Must be controlled, directed and threatened with punishment before they will make any sort of effort
- Prefer to be told what to do and will avoid taking responsibility at all costs.

Managers who fit into this category are likely to rule by making all the decisions, giving orders and threatening punishment.

In contrast, *Theory Y* believes that:

- People enjoy physical and mental effort
- If they are committed to achieving something, people will exercise self-direction and self control
- Under the right conditions, people will accept and seek responsibility
- The vast majority of the population are capable of exercising imagination, creativity and ingenuity.

Managers in this group are likely to be able to involve others in making the decisions that affect them. They delegate responsibility for decisions to the lowest possible level of the organisational hierarchy.

McGregor found that people who hold Theory Y assumptions tended to produce consistently better results than those who subscribed to Theory X. Theory Y is likely to take a positive view of others and will encourage responsibility and trust. Theory X, on the other hand, tends to create barriers because it tries to secure compliance through direction and control, stopping people from becoming independent decision makers.

> Most people's ideas are a combination of X and Y – there's really no such thing as a manager who is completely 'X' or 'Y'. However, if the majority of your beliefs fit into the Theory X category you ought to consider if there is anything you can do to make sure that you are not preventing your team members from achieving their full potential as decision makers.

Decision-making approaches

The two main approaches to decision making are linked to McGregor's X and Y Theories.

- **The authoritarian approach**. Managers assume the authority to take decisions alone and to pass them down the line for implementation
- **The democratic approach**. Here responsibility for decision making is shared between the manager and members of a team.

Between these two extremes lies a range of decision-making processes in which the manager 'sells' the decision to the rest of the team or consults with them before a decision is made. The team's input can be anything from a virtual rubber stamp to a wide-ranging discussion which will determine whether or not the proposal has the support of everyone involved.

The table below shows a range of decision-making methods used by managers. It is based on research by Tannbaum and Schmidt reported in the *Harvard Business Review* (1973). It suggests a continuum of management behaviour: at the top, the style is authoritarian; at the bottom, democratic. The continuum represents a range of action which relates to the degree of authority used by a manager and the amount of freedom available to subordinates in arriving at decisions.

(a) The manager makes decisions and announces them

(b) The manager sells the decision to the team

(c) The manager presents the idea and invites questions

(d) The manager presents a tentative decision subject to change

(e) The manager presents a problem, gets input from the team and then decides

(f) The manager defines the limits and asks the group to make the decision

(g) The manager permits the team to make decisions within predefined limits

(h) The manager allows team members complete freedom of action.

Whichever approach you prefer, you will almost certainly need to judge whether a decision will be acceptable to everyone else. Even if you favour the authoritarian approach, you will still need to sell your ideas to the team and convince them of the value of those ideas. If you fail in this, you may not get the co-operation you need.

Selecting the right approach

Although this book is generally concerned with promoting democratic procedures rather than authoritarian ones, it is important to remember that both perspectives have their place if you want to make effective decisions. A major component of the art of management is to choose the *appropriate* style for a particular task. The right approach for a given situation might be democratic and participative or authoritarian and directive or, indeed, any point on the spectrum in between.

But it is important to note that there are advantages and disadvantages at both extremes of the scale.

- Managers who choose the **authoritarian** approach take decisions rapidly and leave team members free to devote their time to other tasks. They do not, however, use the abilities of the team to the full and members may not feel fully committed to decisions which are imposed on them

- Managers who choose the **democratic** approach encourage team members to feel responsibility for decisions and ensure that everyone gives full consideration to a range of ideas. On the other hand, the democratic process is often slow and cumbersome.

Because good communication is so important within a team, you should encourage and initiate free discussion on a range of work issues. However, the extent to which you involve others often depends upon the matter to be decided. You may feel it would be inappropriate to discuss some decisions – for example, matters of discipline or situations in which you feel it is important to assert your personal authority or opinion.

In reality, it is unlikely that you adopt a single style of decision making. You probably use several of the approaches described at different times.

There are no 'right' or 'wrong' styles of decision making – only those that do or do not succeed in keeping people motivated and committed. The central point is that you should be aware that the methods you adopt must suit the needs of the task in hand, the team as a whole and the individuals within it.

The thinking approach

To make good decisions it is important to first spend time thinking about the problem or issue. Unfortunately, many managers fail to adopt the thinking approach because they feel under pressure to make snap decisions.

When a team member is waiting for you to tell him or her what to do, it is difficult to ask for time to think about it. Or when your own manager is pressing you for a decision, it is all too human to act without much thought so as to remove that pressure as soon as possible.

There are a number of barriers to clear thinking, including:

- **Emotional involvement**. It is perfectly all right to care about a problem, but it is vital to disengage your emotions because they can cloud your judgement

- **Closeness to the decision**. You can get a better perspective on a decision if you detach yourself and try to look at it from a distance

- **Lack of time**. If you find that you are making poor decisions because you are in a hurry, you must reassess your priorities

- **Pressure from others**. You may feel that others are expecting you to be 'decisive' and act quickly. But being decisive means making a good decision – weighing up the evidence carefully before acting – not necessarily a quick decision.

Thinking hard about problems is rather like physical exercise: it seems especially difficult if you don't do much of it, but the more you practise it, the greater the benefits it brings.

It is often quite difficult to think clearly on your own. This is why we advocate involving other people as much as possible. Talking with people and bouncing ideas off them is a great aid to thinking because people who know nothing about an issue can usually see it in a fresh light. In addition, discussion will often help you to change your view of a situation and put problems into perspective.

> Whichever management style you favour, your best decisions will usually be preceded by a certain amount of clear analytical thinking.

The intuitive approach

With all this emphasis on reason and logic it is easy to forget about intuition – those hunches that tell us that a particular course of action is the right one, even though we cannot explain why. The people who choose to ignore their intuition are depriving themselves of a powerful source of wisdom that can be extremely useful in helping them to make decisions. Because the process we are discussing is so complex, it may demand the use of both intuition and reason at different times.

Intuition, sometimes called instinct or 'gut feeling', is something that can give us direct understanding of a situation without any apparent rational thought or evidence. Although intuition does not follow any conscious thought process, it is nearly always based on past experience.

In our culture we have been taught to respect the rational, logical side of our nature and to depreciate or deny the intuitive side. Although we acknowledge the ability of animals to follow their instinct, we are reluctant to admit that human beings have the ability to understand things which are way beyond their rational capacity. However, if we can re-educate ourselves to listen to and trust our intuition, we will be rewarded with much valuable information and guidance for decision making.

> Tapping in to the power of your intuition does not mean that you should eliminate or disregard your rational mind. Your intellect is a very powerful tool that is best used to support and enhance your intuitive wisdom, rather than suppress it.

3

KEY STEPS IN DECISION MAKING

When people make bad decisions it is usually because they have failed to gather all the information they need or to think through the implications of their decisions. In short, they have neglected to be systematic in their approach. A step-by-step approach to decision making was first adopted by the army during the Second World War. It was noticed that officers who used a systematic approach to making decisions had more success than those who failed to impose methodical processes. Since that time managers in the commercial world have adopted these techniques for structuring their thinking and making better decisions.

In this chapter we will examine a five-step approach to making decisions, studying the first two steps – identifying objectives and gathering information – in some detail.

A systematic approach

1. **Setting objectives**. Here you must define the purpose of the decision and consider what outcomes or objectives it will achieve. In some cases these objectives will have to relate to the overall objectives of your organisation

2. **Collecting information**. You must have sufficient information for the choices you need to make

3. **Identifying alternative solutions**. It is important to look at all possible options: some are obvious, others have to be logically deduced; while others require a more creative approach

4. **Evaluating options.** This step involves determining the extent to which the decision options meet the decision objectives defined earlier

5. **Selecting the best option.** After evaluation the 'best' option is selected using any one of a number of techniques or approaches.

We will study Steps 1 and 2 later in this chapter. Step 3 is discussed in Chapter 4, and Steps 5 and 6 in Chapter 5.

Decision-making problems

It is easy to be wise after the event. When things go wrong we can often look back and see what we should have done.

'The trouble is that sometimes I don't think things through enough before jumping in with both feet.'

'It was only afterwards that I realised I'd solved the wrong problem.'

'I got so worried about the decision that I simply couldn't make my mind up what to do.'

'I acted with too little information.'

'I failed to take into account the reactions of other people to my proposed solution.'

'I dithered around so much that by the time I had made a decision it was too late.'

Comments like these illustrate the two most common decision-making problems:

- Acting too fast, or
- Being too slow.

To make decisions successfully and consistently, it pays to take a methodical and systematic approach. If you rush towards a conclusion, you may:

- **Fail to identify objectives**. Neglecting to define the purpose of the decision means that the whole process lacks focus. It is difficult to arrive at a result when you don't know what you want the outcome to be

- **Take a narrow perspective**. You may miss the most effective and appropriate options if you fail to think broadly, logically and creatively about the decision in hand

- **Fail to evaluate the options adequately**. You can easily make a wrong decision if you fail to stop and evaluate each possible option with the utmost care.

If, on the other hand, you are indecisive or slow to make a decision, this may betray a fear of committing to a firm stand. You will feel more confident if you have considered all possible alternatives and the whole range of consequences.

Poor decision making causes frustration, wastes money, reduces morale, weakens commitment and brings about poor performance, so it's worth making sure you go through the process methodically. It may sound laborious, but it gets easier with practice. In the end you will find yourself going through the steps without having to think consciously about what you are doing.

Setting objectives

Identifying your objectives is the most important step of all. Once you are able to focus on your goal, deciding how to get their will be much easier.

There are two types of objectives that you need to be aware of:

- Overall objectives, ie what you want to achieve in the long term, and

- Immediate objectives, ie what you want to achieve by making a particular decision.

Defining overall objectives

The decision you eventually make will be influenced to a great extent by your overall objectives.

- If it's a strategic decision, you need to identify or clarify the organisation's strategic objectives. An example of organisational objectives might be:

> *To excel in anticipating and responding to customer needs*

- If it's an operational decision, you need to consider the objectives of the department or team. An example of overall objectives for a sales team might be:

*To maintain the highest standards of customer
service by providing the customer with the right
products, of the right quality, at the right time,
in the right place and at the right price*

■ If it's a decision that relates to you personally or one
other person, you need to take that individual's long-
or medium-term objectives into account. An example of
overall objectives for an individual might be:

*To contribute to reducing complaints by developing
and refining customer service skills.*

Overall objectives create a challenge and provide a common
direction for people's activities. They are an opportunity to
shape the future. When thinking about the overall objectives of an organisation ask:

■ What is the purpose of our organisation?

■ What business are we in?

■ Who are our customers?

■ Who are our competitors?

■ What resources do we have?

■ What do we want to achieve in one year's (five years',
ten years') time?

When thinking about the overall objectives of a department
or team ask:

■ How do we help the organisation to achieve its objectives?

■ What job are we being paid to do?

■ Who are our customers?

■ What are our budgetary constraints?

■ What do we want to achieve in one year's (five years',
ten years') time?

When thinking about the overall objectives of an individual ask:

- What is the purpose of my/his/her job?
- What contribution can I/he/she make to achieving the team's objectives?
- How does my/his/her work differ from that of other people?

Knowing what the overall objectives are gives you freedom and clarity to make decisions within your assigned responsibilities. You can then:

- See problems in perspective
- Keep going in the right direction
- Stop getting side-tracked into irrelevant and unproductive ventures.

Immediate objectives

Defining immediate objectives will help you to clarify what you want the decision to achieve. It is possible that your objectives may not be the same as those of your colleagues or your manager, so if you want co-operation and support for a decision, it's a good idea to agree your objectives first.

Marina manages a team of production workers in a garment factory. Her team relies heavily on computers and hi-tech sewing machines. One day she arrives at work to find that one of her two computers and several sewing machines are out of action. She soon realises that, unless she does something immediately, they will not meet their deadlines for two important orders and the team will not meet its productivity targets.

The objective of Marina's decision could be one of the following:

■ To find a way of getting the faulty equipment mended

■ To meet this week's orders

■ To keep everyone busy

■ To reach productivity targets

■ To impress everyone with her ability to cope with a crisis.

What Marina eventually decides to do will be very much determined by the way in which she defines her objectives. Because this is an operational decision, she will need to bear her team's overall objectives in mind – these might include 'meeting production targets' or 'ensuring that customers' orders are completed and despatched by the agreed date'.

She would lose sight of these objectives if she concentrates on getting the equipment repaired, on giving everyone low-priority jobs to keep them busy or on looking as though she is in control of the situation. The appropriate choice of immediate objectives may therefore be 'to meet this week's orders' and 'to reach the productivity targets'. She may, for example, be able to hire or borrow some replacement machines, use stand-by equipment or arrange to get the urgent orders completed by another team.

Gathering information

The second step of the decision-making process is to gather information to help you achieve the desired objectives for the decision. To be useful, your information should be:

■ **Relevant**. Irrelevant information wastes time, obscures vital facts, congests information channels and increases administrative costs

- **Supplied in appropriate detail**. You won't need a lot of detail if you are involved in strategic decisions – a broad sweep of information is all that is required. You may need a lot more detail if you are making an operational decision

- **Accurate**. Incorrect information leads to poor decision making. However, you must balance the expense of achieving a high degree of accuracy against the expected benefits

- **Complete**. Like accuracy, completeness can only be judged in relative terms. It would make no sense to hold up a vital decision because the information required was not yet complete. There always has to be trade-off between what is available and what is desirable

- **Timely**. Information is only of use if it reaches the decision maker before the decision is made. It may therefore be better to have information that is slightly less than accurate rather than wait for information that is more accurate but takes a long time to produce.

The gathering of information is usually subject to the law of diminishing returns: at first you may gain a lot of valuable information in a short time, but it will gradually get harder to find facts that are relevant to the decision in hand. While it is a good idea to find out all you can, time and resources will not allow you to collect every last piece of information on the topic. Rather than leaving no stone unturned, you will have to be selective. The value of some items may not be worth the time and effort spent in collecting them.

The questions 'why', 'who', 'what', 'when', 'where' and 'how' are an easy-to-remember checklist of the areas you may need to investigate before making a decision.

If you are making a decision as a group, it is useful to start by brainstorming these questions.

Question	Example questions
Why?	Why did this decision or problem arise? Why do we need to find a solution?
Who?	Who is affected? Who should be involved in making the decision?
What?	What are the true facts surrounding this decision?
When?	When did the problem or issue arise? By when must the decision be made?
Where?	Where did the problem arise? What area is affected?
How?	How can the relevant information be identified? How can it be obtained?

Types of information

There are three types of information that you may need to collect, depending on the decision you are making.

- **External information**. This is the information that flows *into* the organisation from the outside world. Information in this category includes:

  — accumulated information about the market, including customers' requirements and preferences

  — information that gives you clues about the future of the business environment, including facts about the political situation, the economy and social trends

  — information about the plans and performance of competitors

- **Corporate information**. This information *flows* from the organisation into world outside. It includes:
  — marketing and advertising information
  — promotional information that develops the image of the business and helps to sell its products and services
- **Internal information**. This information circulates *inside* the organisation and includes:
  — information about the organisation's plans and objectives
  — facts and figures about the organisation's performance in relation to those plans
- information about income and expenditure.

Traditionally, too much emphasis has been placed on the importance of internal information. Most organisations have only recently become aware of the immense value of external and corporate information for both strategic and operational decision making.

Sources of information

There are three main sources of information for decision making:

- **Human sources**. People are probably your best and most easily accessible source of information. You are probably surrounded by experts in many different fields. For example:
  — personnel officers are specialists in employment law, in recruitment procedures and so on
  — accountants can advise on budgeting and resourcing
  — safety officers can provide information about safe working procedures and risk analysis

— marketing managers understand how to make sure that the goods and services produced by the organisation meet customers' needs.

■ **Written or manual sources**. There may be reports or books that you need to study, journal articles, statistics, letters or in-house publications that you need to read

■ **Information technology sources**. These include databases, CD ROM, and the Internet.

— Databases store data in a way that allows information to be drawn from them in a range of different ways and formats in order to answer a range of management questions

— CD-ROMs (Compact Disk Read Only Memory) look like CDs purchased from music stores, and perform the same function; storing digital information. Vast amounts of information can be stored on CD-ROM disks – annual reports and company information, newspapers, dictionaries, textbooks, etc

— The Internet allows access to such a vast range of data that its usefulness is entirely governed by the sophistication of the systems that sort, filter and present information.

> You can't make a good decision until you know all the facts about the issue or problem at its centre. Once you are clear about your objectives, you need to collect high quality information from the appropriate sources.

4

IDENTIFYING ALTERNATIVE OPTIONS

When you are faced with a decision it is always tempting to select the most obvious option. But sometimes the best solution is not the one that stares you in the face as you contemplate the issue. It is often the creative idea – one of the least apparent answers – that will help to achieve the desired objectives. To be an effective decision maker you have to learn to dig beneath the surface and uncover innovative ideas.

This chapter looks briefly at a variety of ways of identifying options, starting with the logical, rational approach and moving on to look at some more creative tools and techniques.

Listing the options

The third step of the systematic decision-making process is to list all the possible courses of action open to you. You can do this in a rational way if the objective of the decision is clear and you are able to identify specific criteria for the decision.

For example, if you live in the south west of England and you want to get to a meeting in Manchester, the alternative courses of action are:

- Car

- Train

- Coach

- Aeroplane

- Taxi.

Once you have thought of every possible option, you can start to narrow them down by matching them against the decision criteria. Remember, although you should try to find all the options you can, do not assume it is necessary to find every possible alternative. Often there isn't time. For example, you may have to be there by 10 am, you don't want to stay overnight and it would be useful to prepare for the meeting during the journey.

- Never assume your list of options is exhaustive. (Could you get a lift with a colleague, for example?)

- Test the constraints. Are the constraints on your options real? (Do you really have to be there by 10 am?)

- Let your mind run free. Use your imagination to bring more options to mind. (Would it be possible for your client to come to you? Can you organise a video conference?)

- Check that you are not making unnecessary assumptions. (Are there any in-built assumptions? For example, is the cost of the journey really unimportant?)

As you look for alternatives, your mind can easily become trapped by fixed ideas, for example that you have to go there and back in a day, and that you have to be there by 10am. When a problem is particularly tricky, few options may present themselves. That is why it is so useful to go through the earlier stages of identifying objectives, defining the problem and gathering information.

The creative approach

If none of the obvious options look attractive, it may be worthwhile spending time looking for more ideas and information. Finding new ideas may not be as difficult as it is sometimes made to seem; you simply have to use your imagination.

Thinking creatively is a key technique for generating new or different options or solutions to problems. It is the ability to see problems or situations in other ways, to look at them from a different perspective, from another angle – sideways, back to front, even upside down. Creative thinking is in many ways the opposite of the logical, linear way in which managers have often been expected to approach problems or decisions in the past. Despite its value, however, there are many misconceptions about creativity.

- **Creativity is a talent that some people have and others do not.** This is false. Although some people are naturally more creative than others, everyone has the potential to be creative

- **New ideas just happen by accident, it's impossible to plan them**. This is false. It is possible to set out deliberately to generate new ideas

- **Creative thinking has to be crazy to be effective**. This is false. In fact creative thinking is best approached in a rational way and should lead to the generation of ideas that are practical and feasible

- **It is the job of senior managers to be creative**. This is false. In the most successful organisations, senior managers to take the lead in encouraging others to generate ideas and solve problems

- **Only 'clever' people can come up with new ideas**. This is false. Anyone is capable of being creative if they are given the opportunity.

So being innovative is not confined to skilled people, or trained people or 'clever' people – given the right sort of encouragement and the opportunity, most of us can come up with original ideas. However, if this skill does not come easily to you (like most people), you can enlist the help of a range of techniques. It seems like a contradiction, but you can use systematic tools and formal techniques for generating ideas – or, of course, other people. However long one person spends thinking about a problem, sooner or later the ideas dry up. If other minds are available, why not make use of them?

> The creative approach involves using your imagination. Like most people, you are probably creative in some way, and you will have had many original and valuable thoughts about the work which occupies a large proportion of your life.

Techniques for creative decision making

We continue this chapter with a brief description of four valuable techniques that are used within organisations for creative decision making or problem solving. Some of these approaches are more effective if they are undertaken by a group; others can be carried out by people working alone. We look at:

- Brainstorming
- Ideas writing
- Mind Mapping®
- Lateral thinking

Brainstorming

Making premature judgements blocks creativity. We often think of novel solutions or ideas but reject them out of hand because they are too expensive, too unusual, too impracticable and so on. Another block is that of narrow vision; because we are used to seeing things in a certain way, we fail to see alternatives. Brainstorming helps us to overcome both these barriers in our search for new ideas.

The essence of brainstorming is letting your imagination run free – the idea is to break the mould of thinking within confined limits. You can apply this concept even without the help of other people.

The 'rules' of brainstorming are:

1. The leader or facilitator sets the tone of the meeting and explains the problem or decision

2. Participants are encouraged to suggest ideas relating to the problem or situation, and to be as free as possible in their thinking

41

3. The 'scribe' writes down exactly what people say, preferably using a flipchart

4. No interruptions or discussion are allowed, as this interrupts the free flow of ideas and associations

5. When the brainstorm is complete, all the suggestions and ideas are categorised and evaluated. At this point the group draws up a shortlist of the most feasible ideas.

To get an idea of how the technique works, try brainstorming ideas for a fairly unimportant problem. Do this on your own or with a group. Observing the rules outlined above, answer the question, 'What can paper clips be used for?' When you have completed the activity discuss the outcome with your colleagues, using the following questions to help you reflect:

■ How many ideas emerged in the five or ten minutes or so that it took to complete the brainstorm? A long list indicates that you have allowed all ideas to be included – no matter how wild or impractical they may have appeared

■ What about the range of ideas? Groups who have tried this brainstorm before have come up with everything from kitchen gadgets to weapons and from sculptures to jewellery. The more varied your list, the greater the extent to which you have overcome the problem of narrow vision

■ Consider the crazy ideas. Although these might not be feasible, they can often trigger other trains of thought or alert the group to hitherto unexplored areas. For example, although it might be bizarre to think of making jewellery with paper clips, it is perfectly possible to use them as decorative items for toys or as part of a fancy dress costume.

The next step in a real brainstorm would be to cluster the ideas together where possible, so that you end up with groups of similar ideas. At this stage it is perfectly all right to clarify the contributions (What did you mean by . . . ?) although no attempt at evaluation or criticism should be made.

Once the groups of suggestions are sorted out, you can eliminate any that everyone agrees are completely unrealistic. It is important not reject any that are flawed in one area only – it may be possible to make them practicable by extending them or patching them up with other, similar ideas. After a lengthy process of discussion, building, developing and patching, you should end up with a shortlist of three or four options to choose from.

Ideas writing

This technique is similar to brainstorming, the difference being that participants jot their ideas on a piece of paper in front of them instead of recording them on a communal list. It is preferred by people who like to develop their thoughts alone and find working in a group distracting. To stimulate a few more thoughts, an extra list is placed in the centre of the table. When members run out of ideas, they can exchange their own list with the one from the centre.

Some groups note individual items on Post-it notes. The advantage of this system is that Post-its can be displayed for all to see on a whiteboard and easily arranged into clusters. Once they have been generated and clustered, the group moves on to discuss and extend the ideas in the same way as described for the brainstorming technique.

Mind Maps®

Mind Mapping® is a technique devised by Tony Buzan to challenge traditional ways of thinking and listing information. Mind Maps®:

- Build on scientific research into the workings of human brain which has revealed the importance of using colour, images and key words to aid the free association of ideas.

- Involve both sides of the brain – the logical left side and the imaginative right side. Research by neurologists has shown that the left side deals with logic, words, reasoning, numbers, analysis etc., while the right side is linked to areas such as rhythm, images, imagination, colour, daydreaming or patterns.

- Generate information in a form that mirrors the way the brain actually functions, rather than in the vertical, logical lists we are more normally accustomed to. Ideas are therefore shown as coloured images and key words branching out from a central theme.

This is how the Mind Map® opposite was constructed:

1. The creator started with a coloured image of the core subject in the centre – a picture representing the topic about which she had to make a decision

2. She then let her mind flow freely around this image. First she printed the main themes on a thick curved line connected to the central topic

3. Then she added a second level of thought with words or images connected to the main branch that triggered them. These lines are thinner than the main branches and words are again printed

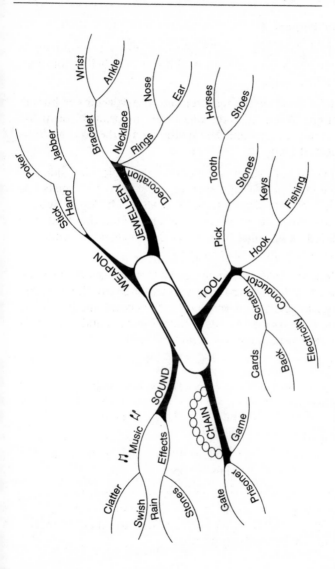

Figure 4.1: *A Mind Map® showing uses for paper clips.*

4. The Mind Mapper® has continued to add third and fourth levels as the thoughts came to her, using images together with words wherever possible.

Mind Maps® allow your brain to assimilate a whole range of interrelated items of information, bringing all the issues into clear focus. They use images and colour, to bring vital creativity to the decision making. The Mind Mapping® process itself often results in or triggers a decision.

Lateral thinking

Lateral thinking is a term invented in 1967 by Edward de Bono. De Bono suggests that, whereas conventional 'vertical thinking' requires you to take up an initial position and then build (or dig down) logically on that basis, 'lateral thinking' allows you to move sideways, to try different perceptions and different entry points.

De Bono suggested many techniques and approaches for finding lateral solutions to problems. Here we describe two commonly used ones: checking assumptions; and six thinking hats.

Checking assumptions

This technique allows us to take a critical look at assumptions that are not necessarily valid. De Bono sees the constraints around a situation as being defined by five factors:

1. **The dominant idea**. This directs the whole approach to the issue or problem. It may be implicit or explicit, for example: 'We sell high quality fountain pens'; or

'This department looks after the well-being of the company's employees'; or ' My job is to process customers' orders and to deal with invoices'

2. **The tethering factors**. These are the factors that tie you in to a certain course of action; they are sometimes quite insignificant. An example could be that a proposed change in employment policy could be tethered because the company has close links with local schools and colleges

3. **The polarising factors**. These are constraints disguised as 'either/or'. An organisation could be either a manufacturer or an importer of finished goods. Polarising factors dismiss the possibility of the halfway house – for instance, a part-finished goods assembler

4. **The boundaries**. These form the framework within which the problem is supposed to be considered. Boundaries can be anything: 'We only sell in the UK'; 'We are a small company'; 'We don't want to issue shares on the open market'; and so on. Boundaries can be real or imaginary, so they should be checked

5. **The assumptions**. Assumptions are the building blocks that created the boundaries so they too should be checked. We must not assume that foreign markets would not be open to us, that the company is not capable of expanding or that no one is interested in a flotation.

Edward de Bono notes that it is never possible to examine all the constraints. Nevertheless, if you set them out logically like this you will become more aware of the 'cage' within which you are operating.

Six thinking hats

This simple but powerful framework is used by many organisations to help people to think creatively when they are faced with challenging decisions. The technique is based on the view that there are six different types of thinking, each one associated with a different colour.

- **White hat thinking** is to do with data and information. White hat thinking asks everyone to focus on the information required for the decision and on how to obtain this. A white hat thinker might say: 'Let's get all the facts straight before we go any further'

- **Red hat thinking** is concerned with feelings, intuition and emotions. The red hat gives people permission to get their feelings out in the open without any need to justify them. A red hat thinker might say: 'I've got a hunch this idea will work'

- **Black hat thinking** is about caution and critical judgement. The black hat is valuable because it helps decision makers to avoid making silly mistakes. A black hat thinker might say: 'The board will never accept this idea because it's too expensive'

- **Yellow hat thinking** is for optimism and taking a positive point of view. The yellow hat looks for benefits and for ways of making ideas work. A yellow hat thinker might say: 'It's true that a new system would take time to introduce, but it would force us to rethink our ideas and our ways of working'.

- **Green hat thinking** makes it possible to ask directly for creative effort. The green hat makes time available to think of new ideas or additional alternatives. A green hat thinker would say: 'Perhaps some new ideas would help; shall we think of some alternatives?'

- **Blue hat thinking** is to do with organising and controlling the thinking process so that it becomes more productive. This hat is usually put on by the chairperson or facilitator of the meeting. The blue hat thinker would say: 'I think we should review where we've got to before we go any further'

Although it is true that some people are naturally more skilled at one type of thinking than another, the coloured hats are not intended to describe the people involved. They refer rather to the type of thinking behaviour that may be appropriate in generating ideas, moving the discussion on or making a decision.

The purpose of the six hats is that everyone should make an effort to wear all six hats as and when they are required to do so by the group. In this way individuals will not become locked into, say, a black hat or a green hat thinking style. The power of the hats is that they allow decision makers to get away from personal arguments and to move towards more objective discussions.

> Whereas logic is concerned with the 'the truth', with what is, lateral thinking is more concerned with possibilities: with what might be. Lateral thinking is also about exploring and changing perceptions and concepts.

5

CHOOSING BETWEEN OPTIONS

This book began by showing that we all make decisions all the time – but that does not mean that we are good at decision making. Yet the process is a crucial one because everything that happens in our work and in our lives is shaped by a decision. The most powerful way in which we can shape the future of a department or organisation is to take action – and before we can take action we have to make a decision.

This chapter deals with the last two steps of the decision-making process: to make a sound decision, you will have to evaluate the different options and then adopt a suitable technique for selecting the best one. In this chapter we discuss how your decisions are influenced by your perceptions, values and beliefs. We also examine a range of methods of actually choosing an option – for example, taking a vote, negotiating or reaching a consensus.

Evaluating options

Once you have generated a number of options, the next step in the decision-making process is to evaluate the most suitable ones. For routine or urgent decisions you may have to take it upon yourself to make this evaluation quickly and informally, using your experience and common sense to guide you. If you worry about having to take personal responsibility for decisions, remember that an average of 40 per cent of decisions taken by managers turn out to be wrong in some way. Only first-class managers will admit this! The important thing is, however, that they actually made the decisions.

For more problematic decisions or decisions that will have a significant impact on the business, however, you will find it useful to approach the process of evaluation more systematically. You could try using some or all of the following evaluation criteria:

- Feasibility
- Acceptability
- Risk.

Feasibility

You can evaluate the feasibility of an option by considering any or all of the following three factors:

1. **The skills required to implement it.** Do you have the required expertise to cope with the implications of a particular decision? Would you have to help existing staff to develop new skills? Or would you have to recruit new people with the required skills?

2. **Its effects on the capacity of the business.** Do you have sufficient human and material resources for the option under consideration? One way of doing this is to

estimate the amount of work that is involved. You can then compare this with your current work commitment to arrive at a picture of the additional capacity that will be required

3. **The financial requirements that would be required**. This is frequently the most important feasibility criterion. Organisations need to know whether or not they can afford a particular option before they accept or reject it. You need to take several different costs into account:

— monetary costs, including one-off costs, running costs and interest on finances that are borrowed

— non-monetary costs: any number of factors could be considered here

— opportunity costs: the costs of pursuing one option rather than another.

Acceptability

The acceptability of an option is the extent to which it fulfils the original objectives of the decision. We examined what these objectives might be in Chapter 2.

For example, if you want to reorganise the layout of an office, you may want to achieve the following objectives:

- A more efficient workflow
- Improved communications
- Space for new equipment
- A more relaxed atmosphere.

The objectives will provide you with some criteria against which you can measure the acceptability of a particular option. The one that you select is the one that meets most of the desired criteria.

Risk

One of the most straightforward ways of analysing risk is simply to assess the worst possible outcome of the option – this is sometimes called assessing the 'downside risk' of an option. If you are willing to accept the consequences of that risk, you can safely go ahead with the option. If, on the other hand, you decide that the downside outcomes would be too great to bear, you would be more likely to reject that option.

Decision modelling is a more sophisticated technique for analysing risk. A decision model organises and formalises the information about a decision, thereby overcoming the subjectivity of different individual perceptions of a problem or situation. Decision models can be created on a computer or drawn and calculated manually. They can take the form of:

- Spreadsheets
- Flow charts
- Network diagrams
- Decision trees.

The simplified example of a decision tree (Figure 5.1 on page 54) illustrates the potential outcomes of a complex decision. In this case, a newly formed partnership providing public relations services is using the decision tree to decide whether to rent premises or work from home.

Personal perceptions

However hard we try to make our decisions objective, it is almost impossible to leave aside our personal perceptions and values. Problems arise because everyone has their own unique perception of how they see the world or a

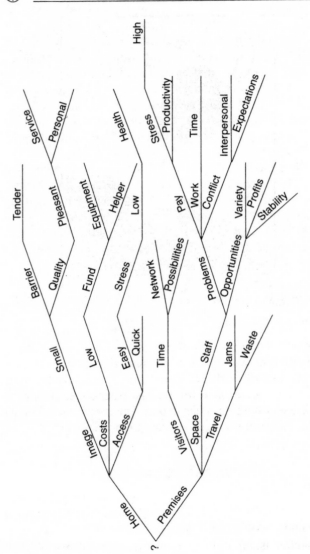

Figure 5.1: *Simplified decision tree.*

Figure 5.2: *Created by W.E. Hill in* Puck, *6 November 1915*

particular situation. Consider for example, the picture above. Do you see a young well-dressed woman or an older poor woman? Or can you see both? It is likely that your response is based on your cultural experiences.

When you have to make a decision the picture that you build up is created from a whole range of factors including:

- Your experiences and intelligence
- Your values and beliefs
- Your personality and interests
- Your aspirations and expectations.

Such factors can lead to your:

- Making assumptions that are based on past experiences

- Screening out facts that do not fit your preferred view of the situation or the decision

- Being blind to the negative (or positive) aspects of a particular decision

- Seeing what you expect to see.

Three managers were asked for their opinion on a proposed reduction in overtime hours:

- The first saw it as a welcome alternative to laying people off

- The second saw it as an unreasonable demand, intended to strip away what staff had come to see as one of their perks

- The third had no objection to this particular move, but was suspicious that it would lead to further cutbacks at a later date.

In order to be as objective as possible when making decisions, it is useful to be aware of the mechanisms you are using to make a judgement about the information that you have collected.

Values

Your values are shaped by your beliefs and your beliefs, in turn, stem from two main factors:

1. Your environment – both past and present

2. Your experience – the success or failure of the things that have happened to you.

It is quite easy to imagine the environments and the experiences that have played their part in shaping the following beliefs:

All individuals have the potential to excel at something

Nothing we can do will alter things

I respect and treat staff as I would wish to be treated myself

Change will provide me and my team with new opportunities to show what we can do

The bosses are only out for themselves – they couldn't care less about front line staff.

When a number of similar beliefs are organised around a particular area of life, a value system starts emerging. Once value systems are established they serve as a powerful force for influencing your judgements and your decisions. Your personal values and beliefs will provide you with a clear focus for your activities, and help you to set priorities in your work.

Organisational values

The importance of clarifying organisational values can be best understood by looking at what happens when there aren't any. There is no common bond, no shared intent and nothing to guide or channel decision making.

A restaurant chain had five senior executives whose values were both unclear and unexpressed. If two of them visited the same outlet to check operations, their reports were often contradictory because each one saw entirely different priorities that needed to be acted upon. Local managers found the reports most confusing because no one knew what priority or strategy would be issued next.

Properly chosen organisational values should:

- Provide a clear focus for decision making
- Create an atmosphere of trust
- Help everyone to set priorities for their work
- Direct training and development activities

■ Reduce politics and games playing
■ Provide guidelines for selecting new employees.

Successful organisations have adopted a strong identifiable set of positive ideals and values which are clearly reflected in their strategies, policies and decisions. The following values are typical of organisations that are continually striving to improve the quality of their goods and services:

■ We look for people who expect the best from themselves and we, in turn, expect the best from them

■ Whether it is customer, supplier or a colleague, we always respect people and treat them as we would wish to be treated

■ We believe that supporting the growth and importance of family and community relationships is important to our business and important in a broader social context

■ All changes to our business must be an improvement to our efficiency and enable us to meet all customer expectations and needs

■ Communication between people is the lifeblood of our business so, as a business, communication should be one of the things in which we excel.

You can evaluate the options you have identified in terms of their acceptability, their feasibility and the degree of risk associated with them. To do this, you will have to be aware of the limitations of your personal perceptions and of the part played in evaluation by your values and beliefs.

Unfortunately, most managers are not consciously aware of the values that they bring to bear on the decision-making process. So you will find it useful to clarify your personal values, and make sure that these relate closely to the values of your organisation.

Selecting the best option

The final step is to choose the best option from the range of possible solutions or decisions you have generated and evaluated. A number of techniques can help you in this difficult task.

Pros and cons

This is probably the most commonly used method of arriving at a decision. It involves listing the advantages and disadvantages of different courses of action, then choosing the one with the most advantages. If, after completing the two lists the decision is still not clear, your next step is to weight the different ideas according to their relative importance, using a scale from one to ten. Add up the totals, and the highest total wins.

The chief executive of a small company is weighing up the pros and cons of moving to larger premises.

- **Pros**: we will have more space for equipment (5); we will be able to take on new staff (8); new offices will make a better impression on customers (8); we will be able to develop our range of services (7); it would be a more pleasant atmosphere in which to work (7)

- **Cons**: soaring costs (9); moving would take up valuable time (6); we would have to neglect our core business for a while (8); the new offices are not so cosy and friendly as the current ones (5).

It is not hard to see which side won in this debate!

If you do the exercise as a group, you can generate a valuable discussion about how you and other managers view the relative importance of the different factors.

Consensus

To reach a consensus you have to keep the discussion going until you arrive at an agreed decision. This approach won't work unless:

- Everyone is honest about their true feelings and opinions
- All participants in have a chance to say what they think
- Everyone leaves the meeting feeling that a decision has emerged as a result of proper discussion and agreement.

Voting

This method is widely used when it is difficult to reach a consensus. You should only use it if everyone present is prepared to be committed to the outcome of the vote.

A group of managers was discussing the colour scheme to be used on the new company logo. Janet preferred the blue and grey, saying that she believed that these colours communicate efficiency, quality and dependability. Roger, for his part, was convinced that apricot and dark red would be better because they stand for humanity, flexibility and desire to treat everyone – both customers and staff – as individuals.

For several minutes the rest of the group watched and listened as the two adversaries locked horns and vigorously disputed each point. The argument continued for several minutes while everyone else listened in astonished silence. Finally, just as it was beginning to look as if there was no way out of the impasse, Anthony suggested that they should take a vote. Without hesitation everyone but Janet voted for orange and red.

Clustering

We discussed the technique of clustering in Chapter 4. It is usually used after a brainstorming session when a group has to deal with a large number of ideas – some of which may be completely wild, while others are relatively mundane. The ideas are clustered into groups – preferably under separate headings or categories. You can then either discard the groups or develop them into workable options. The advantage is that all the promising ideas can be combined or adapted without losing any of them. The final step is to evaluate the group of ideas using one of the other techniques that we discuss in this section.

Negotiation

- If I win, you lose
- If you lose, I win
- If we negotiate, we both win!

Negotiation is a way of arriving at a compromise. It can be used when parties who hold opposing views have to come to a decision that is mutually acceptable. It is often practised in bargaining for pay rises and in the process of bidding for annual budgets. If you adopt this method, you should aim to ensure that one party's losses in one area are compensated by wins in another. The aim of negotiation is to ensure that both parties feel like winners.

You can use questions as a checklist for preparing to negotiate:

1. What do I want to achieve?
2. How far am I prepared to compromise if necessary?

3. What is my fallback position?

4. What does the other side want to achieve?

5. How can I ensure that the other side gets some of the things they want?

A final checklist

Before you take the final step of going public with your decision, check that:

- You are happy about and confident in this decision. (If not, can you do anything about your misgivings?)

- It will be acceptable to your manager. (If not, is it possible to proceed with the decision?)

- It will be acceptable to your colleagues and team members. (If not, how will you manage to persuade them to accept it?)

- It does not set dangerous precedents for future decisions. (If so, what will be the implications?)

- You have given full consideration to all the options. (If not, it is still not too late to think again.)

- You have thought through all the consequences of your decision. (If not, it is worthwhile devoting a little time in trying to foresee the effects of your proposed decision.)

If you have been through a systematic process and asked yourself all the above questions, you can finally come to a decision with confidence.

Implementing and monitoring the decision

Of course, making a decision is not the end of the process. You have to act on it, and then check whether things are working out as you anticipated. There are several reasons why it is important to monitor the effects of a decision once it has been implemented:

■ Monitoring a decision will make your action as effective as possible. It will prove to others that you made the decision seriously and are determined to make it work

■ Decisions often have unforeseen consequences. You cannot always know how a particular action will turn out, or whether your final selection will prove to be the right one

■ Monitoring enables you to learn from your mistakes as well as your successes. Decision-making powers seem to grow with experience and monitoring helps you to improve your decision-making skills.

If a decision turns out badly, it is vital not to blame yourself – we all make poor decisions from time to time, no matter how much thought we give to them. However, it is equally important to admit the mistake and to be prepared to change the decision if it does not work out. In some cases this may mean

■ Revising the objectives of the decision

■ Redefining the problem

■ Gathering more information

■ Finding options that you have not considered before

■ Re-evaluating the options.

Don't be afraid to ask your colleagues and your own manager for help and advice. Being in charge is a lonely job at times and you should look for people who can support you when things go wrong.

Decision-making checklist

We end this book with a final checklist of points to be aware of when making decisions:

- Identify your overall objectives and keep them firmly in your mind
- Be clear about the purpose of the decision
- Adopt the habit of thinking hard
- Don't be afraid to use your intuition
- Be prepared to spend time on collecting high quality information
- Give yourself time to work on a problem
- Be able to differentiate between urgent decisions and important ones
- Involve as many people as possible and use their expertise
- List and evaluate your options
- Talk to your colleagues, friends and family about your problems
- Use all the resources available to you
- Use your imagination – and that of other people – to come up with fresh ideas
- Learn from your mistakes by monitoring the outcome of your decisions
- Make decisions as often as possible – you will get better with practice.